UNDOCUMENTED

Anderson Gomes

DEDICATION

For my two daughters, Adrianna and Caila

CONTENTS

INTRODUCTION

T his book is dedicated to everyone who said a kid who grew up in Brazil amidst drugs, alcohol, and prostitution would never amount to anything.

The stories in this book are real. Some affected me emotionally and some physically, but they are not fiction. They all had a significant impact on my life and shaped me into the man I am today.

We all have a story worth telling, and the events that you are about to read happen to be my story. Never let anyone discourage you from where you are going or what you are doing. Live your life on your own terms.

One of the biggest regrets people have when they get to the end of their lives is what they did not do...the opportunities they missed. Allow yourself to make mistakes, allow yourself to look goofy from time to time. Run your race.

Every time I drive by a cemetery, I think about how many dreams are buried there: how many businesses that never started, how many Amazons that never got off the ground, how many people who could have been the next Steve Jobs. Don't sell yourself short. You have only one life to live.

A special thank you to my wife, Trina, who has supported me through my ups and downs. I would not be the man I am today without her help.

Before we begin digging into my life, it is important to understand that this is not a book based on how bad my life was, nor is it a book to make anyone feel bad for me. Consider this a book to celebrate the struggles: the curveballs that life throws at you. Without the struggles, you can never really appreciate your achievements.

This is a book about how a kid who grew up poor in Brazil, never finished high school, faced many difficulties, but dared to dream...

...a kid who crossed the Rio Grande and lived in the United States for eleven years without a social security card or driver's license, started a business, and now generates over $1 million per year.

This is a book to show you that anything is possible. Regardless of how you define success, whether it be a healthy family, money, cars, boats, or vacations, it does not matter; you can achieve it! You need to believe and take steps toward your idea of "success."

I will not give you a lot of tips or how-tos in this book. It's just my story—and hopefully it will motivate you to push through whatever you are facing in life.

Let's dig in...!

CHAPTER 1

GROWING UP IN BRAZIL

What you are about to read is a combination of events that happened during my childhood. I will show you snapshots of my life and hopefully, at the end of this book, you will see that anything is possible, regardless of your color, financial situation, or where you came from.

EXPELLED FROM PRESCHOOL

My mother signed me up for preschool, which was about a thirty-minute walk from where I lived. There was a limited number of swings on the playground, so at recess I would race to get to them as quickly as I could. After all, it was first come, first served.

There was this little boy who always managed to kick me off the swings. It didn't matter if I was the first kid there or not; he had many friends on his side who would help him.

Finally, I gave up and no longer tried to be the first one to the swings. It got to the point that I was afraid of going out for recess, but there was no option...everyone had to go outside.

Those boys thought they were tough, but little did they know they were not even close to my father back home. I wasn't afraid of the boys; I knew I could stop them if I wanted to. I was afraid of what my father would do if I reacted to the bullies.

My dad was an angry man. I knew if a teacher said anything negative about me, he would make me understand with physical punishment. Only good reports were acceptable, regardless of who was at fault.

After about a month of being bullied, I decided that, regardless of the consequences, I had to make it stop. So one day during recess, I saw Maicon, the leader, sitting on the swing with his friends all around him.

There was a free swing next to Maicon, so I grabbed a handful of sand from the ground and sat on the swing next to him. He stood up and told me to get up. I immediately responded, "No!" His friends surrounded me like a pack of hyenas. When Maicon approached to remove me from the swing, I threw the sand in his eyes. His friends immediately backed off, and the teachers took me to see the principal. The principal sent me home and told me that I was no longer welcome at that school.

At the age of five, I was expelled from preschool. The principal did not call my mother. Instead, I was told to walk home and explain to my parents what had happened.

For three weeks, I didn't say a word to my parents. I left each morning for school and then returned home as if nothing had happened. I hid for the whole five hours school was in session and joined my best friend, Rafael, on his way back from the preschool. Then, Rafael's mother discovered that I was not attending school. She told my mother the entire story. My mother was distraught. How would we explain this to my father?

I knew I would be in trouble for throwing sand at someone's eyes, regardless of what they had done to me. But I had also lied about going to school, which meant I would receive double the punishment.

My father showed no mercy. He pulled out his belt and let me have it. You could tell that he meant business by the way his veins were popping out of his neck, and the bruises that were left on my body.

He did not let me explain anything that had happened. My mother tried to explain too, but if she pushed, he would have hit her as well. Afraid, she turned a blind eye to this and many other situations that were to come.

After getting spanked, I was sore for a few days, but that was nothing compared to the verbal abuse that always followed. It was my father's constant reminders of the wrong I had done and how bad I was that left scars even worse than the beating.

On the bright side, Rafael told me that Maicon and all his friends never bothered anyone again!

❖

IT WAS BEATINGS, NOT DISCIPLINE

My grandmother watched my brother and me many times when my parents could not. Anytime my brother or I did something wrong, my grandma would discipline us. It was not beating; it was discipline.

She would grab a sandal, sometimes even a little stick, and hit us on the butt. It only happened when we did something we knew we weren't supposed to do. It was deserved, and it didn't cause me any emotional distress or leave any bruises.

However, my father did not discipline me. He hit me. Many times a beating would come without any warning, and it was dictated by the way he was feeling at the moment.

He would hit me with a closed fist, belt, extension cords... anything he could find. One time, he even broke a ceramic tile on my head as a form of punishment. He also didn't aim for the butt; he would hit me on every part of my body. The more I moved during the beatings, the more bruises I would have the day after.

There were many days I can recall going to school with welts on my back from my father's beatings. Once, the teacher touched my back, and I flinched in pain. She asked what had happened, and I told her I fell and hurt myself.

ANDERSON GOMES

❖

SOCCER PLAYER

My dad always wanted me to be a soccer player for no better reason than the fact that in Brazil, soccer players make a lot of money.

At school, during recess, we always went to the soccer field to play.

I was always one of the last kids to be picked. I was not good at soccer, and I certainly had no future in playing soccer.

My father would ask, "Why can't you be a soccer player?" Disappointing my father at such a young age was always discouraging.

TOY

A new toy had just come on the market. It was an airport full of little airplanes, gas trucks, and other items found at airports. It was the coolest thing ever.

I asked my dad for one and, after a few months, he managed to get me one. Growing up, we did not have much, so when I got the airport toy kit, I was beyond happy. I was so proud of my airport kit that I wouldn't even dare open the box to play with it. I just wanted to preserve it.

My dad went to see one of his friends at a local pub and brought me along. His friend also had a young son. He saw my airport kit and told my dad that he wanted to buy it. I immediately looked at my dad but was confident that my father would never sell it; he knew how much I cared about the toy.

My dad, at first, showed no interest in selling my toy. After a little while, my dad told his friend that if he convinced me to sell it, then he could have it.

A sense of relief swept over me, knowing that I would never part ways with my prized possession. After a few minutes of negotiation, my dad saw that it was not going anywhere and shot me a dirty look, which meant that I should sell it, and we would buy a new one.

At that point, there was no more negotiation. It was over. I tried fighting for a little, but knew that if I pushed, the consequences would be severe when I arrived home.

Tears poured down my face. I gave the airport to the other boy and explained how it worked. I don't quite know why I took the time to explain it; maybe I wanted to play with it one last time and it was my way of saying goodbye! Or maybe it was because I knew, deep down, that my father would not buy me another one. He did not.

GANG

I was leaving a carnival that was being held in the city I lived in. I left the carnival around 6:00 p.m. with my girlfriend and a couple of friends.

Back in Brazil, we always walked everywhere. We left the carnival on foot and had to walk about seven miles before getting home.

Soon after we started walking, a gang of fifteen guys began walking next to us. Some of the guys looked twenty years old and others no more than eight.

The gang managed to separate me from my girlfriend and friends. After a few minutes of walking, I realized that there was a young kid, about eight years old, next to me.

One of them punched me in the face; another kicked me from behind. My head was down and for another one hundred feet, they kept kicking and punching me. This was a regular practice in local carnivals. If you encountered a local gang, they would typically isolate one person, and provoke them to fight back. If I reacted, I would be attacked by the twenty-year-olds who were waiting behind the young kids.

I didn't react, and they left me alone. They had guns and knives, so responding was not an option.

FIRST GUN

After the interaction with the gang, I called a guy who I knew and bought my first gun. It was a .22 handgun. I was determined that what had taken place the night before would never happen again.

I skipped school many days to practice shooting. I brought my gun to church, school, and any local event.

I remember telling my father that I had a gun and that no one would ever humiliate me again. My dad looked at me and told me to be careful with the gun, that it was not a toy. He seemed to pretend the conversation never happened. After this interaction with my father, I decided to sell the gun.

Looking back at it now, I think the main reason I told him about the gun was that I hoped he would step up and protect me. I was looking for acknowledgment that he would be there for me, but never received it.

YOU WILL NEVER BE ANYBODY

I grew up around a lot of drugs and a lot of bad influences. If you met me back in Brazil, you would have even considered me to be a bad influence.

I never used drugs, but I was always there when drugs were being used by my friends or my father's friends.

Luckily, I never really got in trouble even though I did a lot of very messed-up things. I always felt that God looked over and protected me.

One day, while discussing what we wanted to be when we grew up and what our future would look like, my fifth-grade history teacher said to me, "Anderson, you might as well give up now. Look at your surroundings. Look at your friendships, your parents. There is no future for you. You will either end up in a body bag or jail. Unless you change!"

That was tough for me to hear, but I also knew it was true. If I wanted a future, I would need to make it happen and change many things, including the choices I was making and the friends I had surrounded myself with.

BODY BAG OR JAIL

A lot of my friends died or ended up in jail. In 2017, I lost my best friend, Rafael, whom I had known since preschool. He was a beautiful kid, the sweetest kid you could ever meet. Unfortunately, he got caught up in drugs. One night drug dealers knocked on his window and shot him four times in the face with his two daughters, four and six, standing next to him.

My grandma used to say, "Anderson, lay low. Try to go through life carefully. I hope that nothing happens to you." She would grab my hands and pray. She knew that the probability of me making it to eighteen years of age without getting in some real trouble was very slim.

I knew I had something special to offer. If someone gave me an opportunity, I would take it and not let it go.

FIGHT

One afternoon, my dad and his friends were gathering around our house, drinking and smoking. Most of them were drug dealers or users.

They called my brother and me to the kitchen where they were hanging out, and one of them physically pushed my brother against me. Then the other friend shouted, "You're not going to take that, are you?" The shouting would continue until I pushed my brother back, and then the yelling would turn toward my brother.

After a few minutes, we would be exchanging punches, and the entire crowd would be cheering.

This would go on for about ten minutes before someone would separate us. This happened multiple times throughout the years.

The worst thing was that my parents watched 100 percent of those events without saying a word until my brother or I was on the floor.

My brother and I grew up, eventually becoming strangers to each other. I did not have a real conversation with him until I was thirty years old.

LOST BABY

I was home alone with my brother. My father and mother were coming back from the grocery store in my father's truck.

When they returned, I ran to the truck to greet them. I could hear my dad screaming at my mom. I did not know what the fight was about, but I remember him punching her a couple of times and pushing her out of the truck.

She was several months pregnant. The groceries fell out of the truck onto the ground; there were eggs broken all over the asphalt. My mom was crying and telling me it was OK.

A few days later, she had a miscarriage.

❖

THIS BASTARD IS NOT MY SON

One particular night, at around 3:00 a.m., my dad started screaming at my mother. I wasn't sure what the argument was about, but I knew it was not going to end well. I heard my mother screaming and immediately left my room to protect her.

I saw my father beating my mother. I attempted to stop him by holding his hands, but he was too strong, and he ended up throwing me across the hallway.

I needed to think quick. I started hitting my head on the wall; I would take a few steps back and then run and hit my head.

My dad got irritated and stopped hitting my mother. He went to his room, and my mother helped me.

I went to my room and could hear my dad screaming, "He is not my son; this bastard is not my son. He needs to pack his bags and get out of this house by the morning!"

I was a little over fourteen years old, and leaving home was not a viable option. I did contemplate it, but I didn't see how I could make it work without committing myself to selling drugs or prostitution. I decided to stay.

In the morning he wouldn't look at me or talk to me, but at least he never pushed me out of the house.

I was incredibly proud of myself for stopping him from hitting my mother.

❖

PLEASE DIVORCE HIM

My mother put up with my father. There were not driver's licenses or college degrees for women. My mother thought she needed my father to support us. That's the story she told herself, and she believed it! She worked hard for forty hours or more every single week, but she still didn't think she could do it alone.

Many times she would go to work with a lot of makeup because one side of her face would be all purple from getting beaten the night before.

I asked her many times to divorce him. She always told me she needed him to raise us, and once we were out of the house, she would do what needed to be done. They are still married to this day.

KNIFE

The only people my dad seemed to get along with were strangers and his friends. They always thought that he was the best guy, a good husband and father. But I knew who he was, and spent most of my childhood wishing he were dead. I could not stand him beating my mother, his outbursts, his temper, his aggression!

Several nights before going to bed, I would go to the kitchen to grab a small steak knife and place it under my pillow. I would go to bed, determined to end his life while he was sleeping. I would pray for hours, and slowly talk myself out of killing my father.

I was also fearful that I would be unsuccessful in killing him and would have to deal with the consequences if I failed.

BUSINESSES

Growing up, my father always had different businesses. He had a funeral home, a trucking company, bars, a bakery, grocery stores, food trucks, a liquor store, a newspaper business, and a printing company, to name a few.

I saw my dad starting up and closing many businesses, so I understood the stress that a startup could cause in a family.

I remember praying that my father would find a regular job with paid vacation and benefits, and perhaps he would become happier. Our life was always dictated by the particular business my dad had started at the time. The business would run our lives.

From a very young age, I hated business. I could trace most of my father's outbursts to his businesses. My only aspiration was to get a job and not have the responsibilities or stress associated with running my own business.

Later, I discovered that having a business was not the problem; the main issue was the way my dad operated his businesses. He was never successful. He never developed systems or procedures. He let the business control his life.

One other issue that my father had was his friends. When he started to see some success he would have multiple friends around him, sucking him dry. When the business would fail, his so-called "friends" would disappear.

NAKED

Most members of my family were self-employed. At one point, my grandfather had three very successful bars, among other businesses he owned. One morning my father went to visit his father at the bar and brought me along.

My grandmother went to balance the cash register and noticed that $20 was missing. She assumed someone took the money. When my auntie and my three older female cousins joined us at the bar, my grandmother shared with them that she was looking for $20 missing from the cash register.

My auntie has always been very vocal. As soon as she found out what had happened, she immediately accused me of taking the money. My father started an argument with my auntie that led to screaming and almost became a physical altercation.

At first, he defended me, but shortly after he decided he wanted to prove a point. In front of everyone at the bar, including customers and my three female cousins, he told me to get undressed, so I took my shirt off. He then told me to take everything off. I was hesitant and crying frantically, asking him not to make me remove my clothes in front of everyone. He told me to shut up and do it. I then completely undressed and stood naked in front of every single person.

I couldn't understand how he could so blatantly not stand by me and how he could make me do something so humiliating in front of

everyone. He was trying to prove a point, but in the process, he made this one of the most memorable days of my life.

As it turned out, the money was never missing to begin with. It was simply an error in the calculation.

DRINKING

From the age of thirteen, drinking became a part of me. On holidays, I would ask everybody for a bottle of whiskey or vodka. It was my way of getting away from everything.

Drinking became my best friend for many years.

UNHAPPY KID

When I was a kid, you would look at me, and I would be laughing and smiling, but inside I was a broken kid…miserable.

I saw other people around me who had good parents. I remember praying that my mother would ask me to make my bed, to brush my teeth, to be home early, and other instructions and guidance that good parents provide. I was looking for my parents to show that they cared, but it did not happen.

ENCOURAGEMENT

What carried me through many of my dark moments were the people who said I had something special inside of me.

I would always do things to try to get some positive feedback or validation from people.

One night, while my father and mother were out of town for a few days, I built an entire bar in my room, with a marble countertop and all.

When people looked at it, they would say, "Great job!" or "Wow, you did this yourself? This looks great!" That sparked something within me, and I knew I could and would do something special. I just needed a chance.

There were many other occasions when I did something, and someone would tell me how special I was, how talented I was, how creative I was. They encouraged me; they pushed me forward. I needed validation, and they gave me what I needed.

Never underestimate giving someone positive feedback, especially a child. If they do something, regardless of how small, let them know how special they are, how smart they are. Give them a statement of validation.

I can assure you that that made the difference in my life. I didn't have parents who encouraged me, but throughout the years, many people gave me encouragement that helped me to believe I could do more. This truly helped me become the person that I am today.

PRAYING

In my darkest moments, praying to God is what kept me moving forward. Many nights I would go to bed and ask God to protect and look after me. I would pray myself to sleep.

God has blessed me with more than I deserve!

UNITED STATES

From a very young age, I would tell my friends and family, "One day, I'm going to go to the United States." They would laugh and say, "There's no way! How are you going to make it there? You are crazy!" But going to the United States was my dream.

I was looking for an opportunity. I was looking to get away from everyone and everybody, but most importantly, I was looking for a change.

One day, my dad got sick of hearing me talk about going to the United States and said, "Don't ever talk about the United States again! When you are eighteen, you can do whatever the hell you want. But until then, I don't wanna hear it anymore!"

CHAPTER 2

MAKING MONEY

G rowing up poor, I was always thinking of ways to make money. Some of my ideas were good; others, not so much. Among the many small ventures I started, some stuck with me and actually produced a small amount of income.

POPSICLES

Summers in Brazil are extremely hot. My first business was selling Popsicles on the streets.

I called a local Popsicle company, and asked to rent one of their Popsicle carts. It was a handcart that had two big wheels at the front attached to the cooler; on the back there were handles to push the cart.

The company would fill up the cart at the beginning of the day and whatever I didn't sell, I could return to them.

At the age of twelve, I started my day at 9:00 a.m. and walked the streets screaming, "Popsicle, Popsicle for sale, Popsicle!"

The profit was minimal, about ten cents per Popsicle. On a good day, I would sell a full cart. Eight hours after I started, I made about $3! This doesn't sound like a lot, but it was a start.

❖

COLLECTIBLES

I also tried selling collectibles. I sold old currency, phone cards (compared to baseball cards in the United States), coins, and many other collectibles.

My collectibles business produced enough money to get me through the weekends and invest more into the business. It was never a lot of money, but enough for a kid looking to go out and have a good time on the weekend.

❖

RABBITS

At the age of fourteen, I was given two rabbits and started a rabbit business. They were no ordinary rabbits and definitely not pets. They were larger than a regular house cat.

It was a profitable business. The rabbits reproduced rapidly and before I knew it, I had over thirty rabbits.

Prior to major holidays, people would call me and order a few rabbits. I would kill them, clean them, and sell their meat.

There was only one issue. Where I lived there were a lot of stray dogs who made it nearly impossible to keep the rabbits secure. I had built strong cages for the rabbits, but somehow, the dogs always managed to get to them.

One particular night, a pack of dogs managed to get into the cages and killed every single one of my rabbits. Needless to say, this put me out of business!

CHAPTER 3

MY JOURNEY TO THE USA

T o obtain a tourist visa to visit the United States, you need to demonstrate to the American consulate in Brazil that you are not going to stay in the United States. You can show this by having a college degree with a high-paying job, having rental properties, or owning a successful business...or in my case, I had to demonstrate that my parents had those things.

At eighteen years of age, I had no money, college degree, or assets. My parents also had none of those things. There was no way for me to attempt to get a tourist visa.

The other alternative was to attempt to cross the border from Mexico to the United States.

I did some research, and found a guy in Brazil who was taking people to the United States illegally through Mexico. The entire process cost $15,000. He accepted payments, but the first $5,000 had to be given to him up front.

There was one problem. I had no money. It was a significant holiday in Brazil, so all banks and most other places were closed.

TRUCK

My father had a truck that was worth $15,000. I asked my dad if he would sell his truck, and when I arrived in the United States, I would repay him. To my surprise, he said yes!

MONEY UNDER MATTRESS

My next problem was how to sell a truck when all banks and car dealers were closed. Who would keep $15,000 under a mattress?

My dad mentioned to his uncle that he wanted to sell the truck and he immediately showed interest. My dad expressed his concern in needing the money the same day due to my leaving for the United States through Mexico the next day. His uncle then told my dad that he did not trust banks and that he kept most of his savings under his mattress. I now had the $15,000 that I needed.

FIRST ATTEMPT

I was in my last year of high school and also going to a technical college in the evening. I stopped both and flew from Santa Catarina, Brazil, to Sao Paulo, Brazil, the very next day.

When I arrived in Sao Paulo, I was visited by the guy who was bringing me to Mexico. He gave me instructions, and I flew to Mexico City, Mexico the next day.

I arrived in Mexico and had to go through customs. They asked me what I was going to do in Mexico. They noticed that I was extremely nervous and sent me to a room for a second interview. The room had about twenty-five people from other countries who also had plans to go to the United States.

They called me for the interview where they asked me how much money I was carrying, to which I answered a little over $200. They asked how long I was planning to stay in Mexico; I said two or three weeks. They asked where I was going to stay; I said a hotel. Needless to say, $200 to visit Mexico for two weeks, paying for food and a hotel, would be impossible! They told me I would be sent back to Brazil on the next scheduled flight.

TRYING TO ESCAPE

I could not accept my fate of going back. I could not accept the fact that I was going back to the place I was trying to escape from, right back to the very people who pushed me down.

I came up with an idea. Perhaps if I got sick while in their custody, they would have to send me to a hospital or put me in a different room. I would then attempt to escape and proceed to the United States.

They allowed us to keep our luggage with us in the holding room. I had some pills in my bag in case I got nauseous or had one of my severe migraines. I asked for some water and took six pills. After about forty-five minutes, I started to feel the effects of the pills. My skin turned pale, I began to get sleepy, and everyone around me began to notice as well.

Laying on the floor, I asked for medical services. When they arrived, I was lying there with my eyes barely open. They immediately pulled out an uncomfortably large syringe with a massive needle at the end. I am petrified of needles and, upon seeing it, I started to open and close my eyes to give them the impression I was waking up, and no medical attention was needed. I was fully conscious at that moment. They started to laugh and did not use the needle. The medical personnel asked for assistance to move me to a different room.

I was now isolated from everyone else, and this was my opportunity to escape. I looked around, and the room was empty. I looked for a window, but there was none. I saw a door, which I opened, and from the door I could only see the officer station with about five or six officers blocking the way through it. I watched them for a few minutes and with very little energy left, I lay back down on the floor and waited until they sent me back to Brazil.

Back in Brazil, I could not accept the fact that I did not make it to the United States. I started my research and found another gentleman who brought people to the United States through Mexico, and he put underneath his newspaper ad, "Guaranteed or your money back!" Suddenly I knew this was my opportunity.

❖

SECOND ATTEMPT

I now had only $10,000 left. I contacted the gentleman and told him about the situation. He agreed to take the $10,000, to be paid only if I made it to the United States, and a note in the amount of $5,000. I expressed my concern with the Mexican airport, and he told me not to worry because I would not be stopped. He would take care of everything before I arrived in Mexico.

I was in a group with four other people attempting to go to the United States. Upon arriving at the airport in Mexico, I had to go to customs. This time they did not ask me any questions. They simply took my passport and appeared to have checked my name against a list that the officer had in his packet. He said, "Welcome to Mexico!" and told me to proceed. I could not believe how easy it was. Later, I discovered that the guy in Brazil paid the officers to let us go by without any questions.

Once I entered Mexico, a Mexican guy was waiting outside the airport with our group name written on cardboard. We entered his vehicle, and he brought us to a hotel in Mexico City. He told us to stay there, and we would be contacted by another guy who would bring us to the border for crossing. He also told us not to answer the hotel phone or open the door for anyone, unless it was the guy we were expecting. We were told he would identify himself by saying "USA."

❖

THIEVES, PART ONE

After a few hours, the man showed up and put us in a taxicab. He took another cab and told us we would meet at the bus terminal. On our way to the bus terminal, we got stopped by the Mexican police.

They told us to give them all the money we had in our pockets. We knew we needed money to buy bus tickets, but had no option. We gave them all the money we had. One of the police officers took my sunglasses from my head and put them on his head. At this point, we had already paid for the taxi. It seemed like the taxi driver knew the officers, and it was all premeditated.

THIEVES, PART TWO

At the bus station, we were all just looking at each other and trying to figure out how we were going to pay for bus tickets. We needed to get to Guadalajara, Mexico, where we would, be met by yet another person who would bring us to Laredo, Mexico.

Luckily, one of the Brazilian guys we were traveling with had put some extra money inside his socks and had enough to pay for all of us.

The Mexican guy from the hotel met us, and off we went to Guadalajara.

On our way to Guadalajara, we were stopped by different police officers. They entered the bus and asked us to exit. They demanded money. None of us had money, except for one guy. They took all his money and let us proceed.

HOLDING HOUSE

When we arrived at Guadalajara, we were met by a guy who told us to get in his truck. We proceeded to Laredo, where we stayed at his house with his wife, his daughter, and her boyfriend.

They said that the only way for us to get out of their home and proceed to the United States would be to pay their fee. Most of our money was with the Brazilian guy who started the process back in Brazil. He was not answering his phone, and we were stuck!

DESERT

When the money finally arrived, and we were scheduled to cross the border that same night. They told us that if we wanted to carry a small bag with some clothes, it would be OK. Everything else had to stay at the house.

The Coyotes—that is what the Mexican guys were called—went to the store and bought water bottles and vinegar peanuts. They said it would help.

We went under a wire fence and saw a desert that appeared to be never-ending. We walked for two days.

The nights were long and extremely cold; the days were short and extremely hot. We were all hungry and proceeded to eat the vinegar peanuts, which made us very thirsty. It was not long before all the water and peanuts were gone.

In retrospect, I believe that was their plan all along. If we were weak and hungry, we would be more easily persuaded to follow their guidance.

After two days of walking, we had to cross the river, the infamous Rio Grande, which was an extremely difficult feat. The water was freezing, and we had no clothes to change into after crossing. The river's current was very strong, and we could barely keep up. I knew that if something happened, there would be no rescue attempt. If someone had gotten hurt and could not keep up, the person would be left to die. Luckily, we all made it across the river.

TRAIN

We were all wet, hungry, and freezing. We lay next to each other in an attempt to warm up while we waited for a cargo train, which was supposed to cross the desert at a particular time. When the Coyotes saw the train, they screamed for us to run, run, run!

The train was about three hundred feet from where we were; it was moving at a speed of approximately twenty miles per hour. We had to catch the train while it was moving. One by one, we went up to the side ladder to jump inside the cargo container.

We rode the train for approximately three hours until it suddenly stopped. The Coyotes told us to put our bodies against the side of the container because the train operators were about to perform an inspection.

We were all silently praying and hoping they wouldn't spot us. I had my eyes closed, and I could still feel the light of their flashlight burning holes through me. Shortly after, I heard two big bangs on the side of the train, and suddenly it started to move.

After another three hours, we finally arrived at a secure train station in the United States. The Coyote told us to get up and get ready to jump. I opened my eyes, and the first thing I saw was a huge American flag. It was the most beautiful thing I had ever seen and, to this day, one of my most memorable moments.

We were all ready to jump. I was the last one to go and, without hesitation, I jumped. Instead of jumping in the direction the train was going, I jumped in the opposite direction, causing me to roll backward and hit my head. I passed out for a few seconds.

When I opened my eyes, I could see the train rushing by no more than one foot from my head. At that moment, I realized I could have died; I couldn't help but feel that God was truly looking after me.

All I could hear were the other Brazilian guys and Coyotes screaming at me to get up and move. I immediately gathered myself and rushed over to them. They were all behind some bushes that were located a few feet from the train track.

SAFE HOUSE

We walked to an auto body shop that was close by; the Coyotes seemed to know the owner. They instructed us to go under a tractor trailer and stay there until they told us to move.

We stayed underneath the tractor trailer for what felt like an eternity, unable to get up for anything. If someone had to use the bathroom, they were forced to go in their pants.

Eventually, after a full day of enduring the elements, the Coyotes got an SUV and brought us to a house nearby.

Once we arrived at the house, we were told not to get comfortable, as we would be transported to another location soon. The final payment was pending. Nevertheless, we were finally able to use a bathroom, drink water, and eat our first meal of the trip.

After a few hours, we were transported to a house in Houston, Texas. We were not allowed to leave the house, but we were able to shower, use the restroom, and have food and drinks as we pleased. We stayed at that home for two days.

Once the final payment was made, we were free to go to our destinations. We rented a van and all went to Boston, Massachusetts, where we knew there were a lot of Brazilians. This would make finding a place to stay easy.

WAS IT WORTH IT?

The journey was long and by no means easy, but I am proud of my story on how I arrived.

I feel many people born in the United States take for granted how lucky they truly are, never realizing that being born here is like winning the lottery.

If I had to do it all over again, I would without hesitation.

CHAPTER 4

IN THE UNITED STATES

I arrived in the United States and the first six months were tough. I didn't understand the culture, and I didn't speak English. All I wanted was to go back to Brazil.

For the first time in my life, I saw division; people were categorized and put into groups. There were Chinese, black, white, Brazilian; categorized by color, race, and ethnicity.

In Brazil, a lot of my friends were black. We never saw them for color, race, or ethnicity. I never had to think about myself as being Brazilian until I got to the United States. I was titled the "Brazilian kid." It was very confusing to me.

I wanted to return to Brazil, but I didn't have money to go back. I called my parents several times complaining. One day my dad said,

"Pack your bags and come back if that's what you want to do. But never talk about the United States again."

I now had options and in that very moment when he said, "Pack your bags and come back," I realized I wanted to stay. I needed to prove to myself that I could brave this hard time and make it work. I also owed money to my dad and knew I had to pay it back.

The alternative to staying was to go back to Brazil…to the very place that I had escaped from.

❖

MY PLAN

Once I decided to stay in the United States, I developed a plan. My plan was to work hard for five years, pay my father back, and buy rental properties back in Brazil. After the five years, I would return to Brazil and continue my life there.

I had everything figured out, so now, I needed to put my plan in action.

❖

ACCOMMODATIONS

When I arrived in Boston, without money, I lived with five other male roommates in a two-bedroom apartment. There was no privacy and no sense of ownership.

My roommates were all from Brazil. Inside the apartment were Brazilian flags; all the TV channels were Brazilian; all the music they listened to was Brazilian; everything was in Portuguese. It was like I never left Brazil. I wanted to learn to speak English and learn about the culture, which seemed nearly impossible in these conditions.

On a nightly basis, one of my roommates would get drunk and snort cocaine. One of them made and sold fake documents such as social security cards, work authorizations, green cards, and other documents that would generate buyers. Another roommate sold stolen items like computers, cell phones, and other items that could be easily sold.

To me, all that was very normal; it was like I never left Brazil. It was all in my comfort zone because I knew the type of people I was dealing with.

I knew I left Brazil to start a new life, a life based on integrity and values. Living with those roommates made it seem like I had never left. I was still surrounded by the same type of people and living in the same kind of environment I had been trying to escape.

I concluded that I attracted only the same type of people. To change this, I would need to change my surroundings, and most importantly, I would need to change myself first.

STOLEN COMPUTER

One of the first things I did when I arrived in the United States was to buy a stolen computer. I bought the laptop for $300. It was brand new, and I was proud for a brief moment.

I then realized that I was doing the same things I had done back in Brazil. For things to change, I had to change.

I called the guy who sold me the stolen computer and asked him to take it back, which he refused. I then told him to take the laptop back and keep the money I had paid for it.

He picked up the computer, and that was the last time I ever purchased a stolen item.

FIRST JOB

My very first job was working for Comcast through a subcontractor. It was a good-paying job.

I would climb light poles to remove a small filter that was interfering with some TV channels, which had been discontinued. I worked in the Boston area and, because we worked outside, it was brutal during the winter months.

We were getting paid $3 per filter. We could work as many hours as we wanted.

The owner of the company that subcontracted to Comcast was a Brazilian man. He was not paying his bills. He was doing a lot of shady deals and, to stay out of jail, he had to escape back to Brazil.

None of the employees were paid, and I now needed a different job.

OLIVE GARDEN

Finding a job was a challenge. A brand new Olive Garden was opening up in Marlboro, Massachusetts. They had just finished construction, and they were hiring line cooks, dishwashers, servers, and staff to open.

I applied and they said no. I applied again; they said no. I went there for the seventh time. The guy who had conducted interviews with me before saw me and said, "Listen, I don't know if we are not understanding each other. Do you need a translator?" He called a guy who spoke Portuguese and said: "No, tell him no, no more, tell him not to come back!"

The general manager saw the interaction, approached us, and asked, "What is the deal here?"

He explained, "This kid has come back seven times, and I told him no!"

She said, "If he came back seven times maybe he wants the job!" After much perseverance, I was hired to be a dishwasher.

As a kid, I had built up a lot of anger, and now I was able to channel those emotions into my work. People who told me I couldn't do it now became fuel for the fire within me. I could work longer and harder than anyone. I was determined to become the best dishwasher they'd ever had!

I would be washing dishes, organizing all of the plates and silverware, singing, and having fun.

Anyone who has worked in a restaurant knows that most of the waiters and servers throw dishes at the dishwashers and move on. They wouldn't even have a chance to throw the dishes; I would catch them and proceed in organizing everything perfectly. The managers would walk by me and say, "Oh, wow! Great job! Great job!"

The guy who denied me employment would look at me and keep walking. I would think, "Yeah, you are the one I wanna prove wrong."

After a few hours working as a dishwasher, the woman who gave me the position promoted me to cooking pasta. I was so happy! It felt as though they had given me the restaurant to run.

They would say, "You gotta weigh the fettuccine; five ounces for lunch and eleven ounces, twelve ounces or whatever the case is for dinner." If I had 5.1 oz, I would cut a fettuccine in half...I was a perfectionist.

I stayed in the pasta stations for about two days. Then they promoted me to learn the entire prep station. Shortly after that, I was promoted to learning how to be a line cook.

At this point, the guy who denied me work was my best friend because I was the go-to guy.

They promoted me to a certified trainer. This meant they gave me a gas card, put me up in hotel rooms, and I was going to experience traveling throughout the United States opening new Olive Gardens. It was an excellent promotion, and I was proud.

My girlfriend would come to my hotel room, and we spent most nights drinking beer and translating the handbook.

I was a pain to the managers because I was uncertain if I was ever good enough. I was so used to always being pushed down, so my confidence level was very low.

I would be cooking pasta and then something would click in my head. "Am I doing this good enough, quick enough?" I would go to the manager's office and ask, "How am I doing?" They would tell me, "You are doing a great job, keep on going." I would work another hour and say, "Wait a minute; I gotta go ask them again." So I would go to the door and knock again.

It came to the point that as I approached their office they would open the door and immediately say, "Anderson! You're doing great! Keep on going!" and that was all I needed to hear.

I would go in to work at six in the morning and wouldn't leave there until three or four o'clock in the morning. I would sleep for two hours or less, get up, and go again. I did this six days per week, sometimes even seven. My paychecks were sometimes bigger than the managers'. I was working an average of 110 hours per week.

Olive Garden was the first place that believed in me. The managers would tell me that I was great. Many times they would ask if there was anything they could do for me. One day they offered me more money, but I told them to keep it. All I needed was to be told that I was doing a great job…I needed encouragement.

When my coworkers discovered that I refused the raise, they called me crazy. But I knew that encouragement did a lot more for me than money.

❖

MEETING MY WIFE

Olive Garden also gave me the most valuable gift of my life. It is where I met my wife. Trina was a hostess at Olive Garden. She was going to Framingham State College and, to help pay for the expenses, she was working two jobs while attending school.

From time to time, I would see her walking by my station and would look at her. She would look back and smile. She has a beautiful smile.

I would be looking at her through the window that connected the kitchen to the front of the restaurant. After a short while, it became noticeable to everyone that I was interested in her, but I thought I had no chance!

One day I made a wager with a Brazilian guy to see who would get Trina's number first. He attempted…but nothing, she would not budge. Neither one of us spoke English. It was a challenge to hold any conversation, let alone get a girl's number.

I attempted and somehow she understood me. She asked my age, so I asked, "What is your age?" and she said twenty-three. So I replied that I was twenty-three, as well. In reality, I was only nineteen, but I didn't want to ruin my chances.

I managed to ask her if I could come over to her place. She said yes! I told her I would follow her after work. Without a license, I proceeded to follow her. She lived only about twenty minutes from Olive Garden.

Trina drove way above the speed limit; I think she had intentions of losing me, but I was persistent. I never drove even one mile above the speed limit because I didn't have a license and a simple traffic stop could lead to my being deported.

I arrived at her apartment, and we spent the night talking, or at least, trying to! She pretended she understood me. We drank a couple of beers and had a great time.

Before things became serious, I felt obligated to tell Trina I was living in the United States illegally. I didn't feel it was right to pursue the relationship without her knowing the truth. She was very accepting of my situation, and it didn't seem to bother her at all.

Discovering my real age bothered her way more! She was shocked and even cried. She could not believe she was falling in love with a guy who technically could not even have a drink.

This was the beginning of a lifelong relationship that developed into marriage. After a few months of dating, I moved into Trina's apartment.

Trina came from a good family who cared for her, and they taught me many lessons. It truly helped me become the person I am today.

Trina showed me a different life. She had a lot of compassion for my past and, at the same time, pushed me to become a better person. She was and is, to this day, a strong person who has always made it clear what she would and would not put up with. This was exactly what I needed: someone who would push back, not push me down!

❖

LANDSCAPING

I was looking for a second job and found a local landscaping company that was hiring. I asked for a job, and they said yes. They assigned me to a supervisor, and he brought me to a job site.

He gave me a leaf blower and asked me to clean up a yard full of leaves. I had about three to four hours to get this job done and thought it was enough time.

Every time I blew the leaves, they went backward. I was determined to get every single one of them. I couldn't leave one behind, but every time I went to blow one, another one flew back.

It was a particularly windy day, and I was there from eight in the morning to seven at night, yet the job was not completed. I was sweating and fighting with the leaves. It was comical.

Landscaping was not for me. I told the supervisor to keep the money since the job was not done to perfection.

That was my first and last day in the landscaping business.

RENTAL PROPERTIES

While working at Olive Garden, I was still thinking that one day I would go back to Brazil. I knew I could be deported at any time, so I needed to have some investments in Brazil just in case.

I worked hard and was able to put money aside. I would send all the extra money I had to Brazil. In a little over a year, I was able pay my father back for the original investment he made in financing my trip to the United States and was also able to purchase a house and two pieces of land in Brazil.

My family was super happy that I was making progress. But then things started to change!

OLIVE GARDEN - THE END!

I had been working for Olive Garden for two years, and I overheard the managers saying that they were going to promote me to a management position in Jamaica Plain, Boston. I was extremely happy; I had worked so hard for that!

But then I realized...I can't be a manager; I am an illegal alien! I wasn't sure if I was going to stay in the United States or be deported to Brazil. I couldn't fly out of the country. I didn't have a social security number or a driver's license.

To become a manager, you have to fly to Italy and attend a culinary school that Olive Garden has. Then you fly to Florida for graduation.

I called my district manager, and I opened up to her about my being illegal. She asked me who else knew about the situation. I told her that no one knew, but I loved Olive Garden, and I understood that she needed to follow the rules and let me go. I explained that I had certain rules I upheld, and I've done so for two years, so I would never ask her to break them. She was crying while I managed to compose myself. I shook her hand and left. That was the last time I ever worked for Olive Garden.

It was like I lost everything. I even contemplated taking my life. I looked up and said, "God, why all the struggles? I thought moving to the United States would be different. Why me?"

For two years had I worked so hard. I had lived and breathed Olive Garden. It was the first place that believed in me, and now it was gone!

CLOSED DOORS

God knew exactly what he was doing. Today, I thank God every day for closing that door, because I learned to trust in God a lot more. When he closes a door, another one will open; you need to have faith!

We always think that things happen to us. When they don't, they happen for us.

When going through a difficult time, we see what is happening right in front of us, but there is so much more. It's like having horse blinders on. You can only see what is in front of you, but once the blinders are removed, you can see the whole picture.

FINANCIAL STRUGGLES

We didn't have credit cards back in Brazil, not like in the United States. I came to the United States and about three months later started receiving credit cards in the mail. I maxed out every single credit card that arrived at my door. Before I had even realized, I had over $30,000 in credit card debt.

After I left Olive Garden, I couldn't afford to pay for my truck or credit cards. Trina and I also discovered she was pregnant.

Trina was born in Alaska but lived her whole life in Agawam, Massachusetts. We were expecting our first daughter and decided to move to Agawam to be closer to her family.

BEFORE MOVING TO AGAWAM

Before moving to Agawam, I tried getting a job at a local seafood restaurant. I worked there for one week, and they discovered I was living in the United States illegally. They did not want to fire me, so they offered to pay me under the table in cash.

At this point in my life, living with Trina, I had started the process of changing my life and doing things only by the book. So, I denied their offer.

They attempted to pay me for the week I had worked. I told them I could not accept the money.

Even being illegal, I applied to serve in the United States Army and obtained an ITIN number with the IRS. This allowed me to pay my income taxes since the first year I arrived in the United States.

GETTING MARRIED

Before having our first baby, Trina and I wanted to get married.

We decided to have a very small ceremony because we feared her family would not approve, so we kept it a secret.

We also thought that by getting married, my immigration situation would be solved quickly, and we could move on with our lives without fear.

We obtained a marriage license. There was only one problem— the rings! We were broke, so buying rings was going to be challenging.

Trina and I went to several stores looking for fake diamond rings. We found several, but it was not what I wanted to give her. I called a local Brazilian jewelry store and asked them if they financed. They said yes! I went and picked up two rings for a little over $1,200.

We called a justice of the peace to our apartment and right there, with Trina and me standing in the kitchen, we got married.

AGAWAM

In the Agawam area, I worked for two local restaurants, but they were no Olive Garden. It was a tough thing for me to get over. At Olive Garden we had to wear gloves, we had rules; they were very professional. The restaurants I was now working at were not the same; rules were not enforced.

My wife got a job at Bob's Clothing Store, in Manchester, as a manager. She was bringing home some money, but we had so much debt that it seemed impossible for us to catch up.

The week that my daughter was to be born, I quit both of my jobs. We were living in Agawam, paying a little over $700 per month in rent. We were able to afford it with her job and my two jobs at the restaurants. But now I quit both jobs because I wanted to do more!

Working at Olive Garden, I saw many of my coworkers coming into work and saying that they hated their job. They would leave with the same attitude. I never understood. No one was holding a gun to their heads and telling them to stay there. I loved my job, but they were unhappy. I would say, "You are not a tree, you can move. Find another job!" But they would not. Many of them are still employed at Olive Garden to this day.

I decided that this would not be me. I was unhappy working for the other restaurants and decided that life is too short, especially when it comes to a job. This is why I had to quit!

CHAPTER 5

STARTING A BUSINESS

Having my own business was something I never envisioned or even wanted because of my firsthand experience regarding how business can affect family life.

So I fought against the thought of having my own business. But the more I fought, the more I was drawn to the idea of trying something. I didn't necessarily want a particular business, I wanted to start something in which I could impact lives, create lasting impressions, and that had the potential to make an endless amount of money.

I have never been one to call out in any of my jobs. Even if I were sick, I would still go to work and get the job done. I always showed up on time and left a little later to ensure I did my very best work. Regardless of the job at hand, I was continually thinking of a better way to do the job. I was used to working a minimum of seventy hours per week, so I figured if I applied my work ethic toward something that was mine, I would reap the benefits.

I was also living illegally in the United States without paperwork. This made finding a high-paying job difficult. I did not finish high school, nor did I have a college degree.

So the decision was made...I had to go into business for myself. Regardless of the business, I needed to try something.

CLEANING BUSINESS

I was sitting on the couch thinking what could I do that didn't require a lot of money to start. I needed a business that would allow me to evoke emotion from people in such a way that I would be rewarded if I did an outstanding job...a business where I could have employees and impact their lives positively...a business that would have unlimited income potential. That's when the idea of starting a cleaning company was born.

I put a free ad on Google for a company that I named LookClean Commercial Services. I did not have to spend one penny.

A week went by, then two weeks, and now my wife was starting to pressure me to bring home the bacon. The bills were starting to add up, and the arguments began.

The worst arguments are always about money. We had this bill and that bill. Which ones were we going to let go, which ones were we going to pay?

I was extremely miserable being at home and not providing for my family, but I didn't want to go back to restaurants.

Three and then four weeks went by; the arguments intensified. One day, after a bad argument, Trina said, "You have to go get a job."

And I finally said, "OK, I'm going to go back to the restaurant business."

CHAPTER 6

FIRST ACCOUNT

I went to call one of the restaurants I had worked for and noticed I had a missed call and the following voicemail: "My name is Janice Leary. I fired my cleaning company, and I am looking for cleaners. I called several companies, and no one is calling me back. Can you please call me back?"

My wife was at work. I called her and said I didn't feel comfortable calling the potential customer back. I didn't know if she was going to judge me by my accent. Trina called Janice Leary and scheduled a meeting for the very same day.

I also didn't want to go by myself, so Trina took time off from work and came to pick me up while her mom watched our daughter.

When we saw the building, it was huge—150,000 square feet. As soon as she pulled into the parking lot, I told Trina to keep on driving. "Keep on going. I'm going to go back to the restaurant…this business was a bad idea."

She said, "No! I'm not. Listen, I took time off from work. I put my suit on. There's no way we aren't going in!"

I become agitated and said, "Listen, are you gonna clean this? You're not! So keep on driving."

She parked the car, took the key from the ignition and started walking toward the entrance. We wouldn't even look at each other. I was very concerned and overwhelmed by the size of the building and the meeting that was about to take place.

FIRST MEETING

Janice Leary showed us the building and asked, "Do you provide carpet cleaning? Strip and wax floors? Window cleaning? Upholstery cleaning? Do you have worker's compensation? Liability insurance? Is your company bonded?" I said, "Absolutely, yes!" to all of her questions.

I didn't have experience performing any of the tasks she asked me, nor did I have insurance. I didn't even have a company on paper yet.

However, what I did have was the confidence that I cared and would always do my very best. I would do whatever it took to learn anything needed to perform my job well. A person who cares without knowledge can surpass anyone with knowledge who doesn't care.

WHY THE OTHER CLEANER GOT FIRED

During the walkthrough, we went to the basement. There were several trucks parked by the loading dock that were unloading furniture and computers. I asked Janice if they purchased new furniture. She said, "No, that was the furniture that the former cleaning company had stolen from us." Janice said that they had a storage room and, throughout the years, multiple pieces of furniture went missing. They decided to install cameras and discovered that the cleaning company had been stealing from them.

I asked, "If everything goes well, when would you like us to start?" She said, "Tonight would be great." It was a twenty-four-hour facility, and they had 280 employees, so there was a lot of trash accumulating. She asked us for a proposal, and I went home to start crunching numbers.

PRICING

One of the toughest things in business when you first start is pricing jobs. If you price too high, they may think you don't want the job in the first place or that you don't know what you're doing. On the other hand, if you price too low, they may think you did something wrong or that you're trying to rebuild, you're desperate, and again, don't know what you're doing. I had done copious amounts of research and finally came up with a price.

They wanted me to clean six nights per week, about three hours per night. But before I gave the price, I had my wife call and ask how much they were currently paying for cleaning services. Trina was doubtful she would be provided an answer, but she called Janice Leary anyway.

She told Trina what she was paying, and it was so much more than what I was about to charge! When my wife told me the price, I contemplated lowering it but decided to raise the overall monthly price.

My wife was worried that we would lose the opportunity and asked if I was crazy. We had no money, I had no job, we had a lot of bills to pay, and I was just about to gamble with our first real opportunity.

I asked Trina to tell Janice Leary that the price needed to be raised $100 per month. Trina called, and Janice said "OK. Where do I sign?" and requested proof of insurance.

PAPERWORK, SUPPLIES, AND UNIFORMS

Now I needed a company on paper. Since we had only one car and my wife had to go back to work, I called my mother-in-law to pick me up. We went all around Agawam and in one hour and $25 later, I had an ITIN number, bank account, and business certificate; everything was legit.

There was only one problem. I needed insurance and had no money! I went to a local insurance company, did all the paperwork, and asked, "How much money do you need for a down payment?"

He said, "Don't worry about it. You can pay me later."

I needed supplies and equipment, so I called my father-in-law to help. He let me borrow $1,500 on his credit card. After a little over an hour of shopping, I was all set to start.

From day one, I always wanted to have uniforms. We were supposed to start cleaning that evening, and I did not have time to order company shirts. Trina went to Walmart and bought iron-on letters and a few blue T-shirts. We made T-shirts with our company name, and I was ready!

Janice Leary signed the proposal, and that very night I was officially in business.

❖

CLEANING NIGHTS

The agreement was to clean the site six nights per week for about three hours per night. I worked seven nights per week for about twelve hours per night. I would go in around 8:00 p.m. and leave around 8:00 in the morning.

Why was I working so much more than what they were paying for? I was investing in my business. I felt that the site was so big and there were so many variables. There was so much that I could learn. I felt like I should have paid them for all the knowledge and experience I took from it.

❖

BUILDING GOOD RESERVES

In life, what helps you get through the bad times are the good memories you have built; I refer to this as building good reserves. There will be negative moments that bring you down, but it's the good experiences and memories that help you see the light at the end of the tunnel. The good reserves need to always surpass the negative moments—the mistakes.

It is no different in business. I knew I was new to the cleaning business and was going to screw up. When I did, I wanted them to think about the good reserves I had built, the good "moments" we had together. The good reserve was me giving them seven nights per week, twelve hours per night. What other company would ever compete with me? When I screwed up, I wanted them to think about that.

USING THE GOOD RESERVES

They asked me to strip and wax the cafeteria floor. You have to use a side-by-side machine that rotates 175 rotations per minute... so it's a slow machine. I went to Taylor Rental and told them I needed to strip a floor. They gave me a high-speed burnisher. It rotates 2,000 rotations per minute, a very fast machine.

When I put that fast machine on top of the floor chemical, it splattered all over the walls, cabinets, etc. A day after the job was completed, the floor looked worse than before.

Every single time I screwed up, they looked the other way. I was giving them so much more than what they were paying for. I had built so much good reserve, that it was nearly impossible to use all of it.

I did not charge them, but I did go back and repeated the job, days later, with much more success and with the proper equipment.

RECESSION

I started my business in late 2007, right when one of the worst recessions in the United States since the Great Depression was about to begin.

My first account was an international company based in England. They were doing very badly financially. They cut all their employees' pay by 10 percent, and they were unable to pay me.

NO PAYMENT

Thirty days went by without pay, and everyone around me said, "You tried. You gave your best. Just let it go, give up. There's nothing wrong with giving up."

Sixty days went by without pay, and my wife started to get worried. She told me that if I continued with the business, working seven days per week, twelve hours per night, not getting paid, and not providing for the family, it would likely end in divorce. She asked me to go back to the restaurant because $200 would be better than nothing.

I told her if this business ends up to be nothing, we have not lost anything, or it's going to end up to being something. Thirty, sixty days without a check was nothing compared to what I went through back in Brazil. The check was just a piece of paper.

DOLLAR ICE CREAM

It was a sunny day, and we were looking for a dollar to buy our daughter an ice cream at McDonald's. We looked everywhere, but we were able to find only ninety cents.

I was looking down from our second-floor apartment to where my wife was turning her Ford Focus upside down looking for that last ten cents that we needed.

When Trina came upstairs, she was so angry. Angry at me, at the whole situation, when suddenly that anger turned to tears.

With tears pouring down our faces, we hugged and asked each other, "What if we can find the extra ten cents, do they charge tax?"

We were not able to find the extra ten cents, and we were unable to buy my daughter an ice cream.

That was one of the moments that fired me up, and I said: "I gotta make this thing work." Instead of going to work depressed about the ten cents, I would work ten times harder than the night before. I needed to make it!

MOVING IN WITH MY IN-LAWS

We could no longer afford our apartment; we packed our bags and moved in with my in-laws.

Close to ninety days went by without pay. That was tough. Everybody around me lost all understanding and started to call me crazy. They were telling me to give up. They went from being understanding and soft to aggressive and extremely persuasive.

My wife would look at me, and I could tell she was extremely disappointed. She would be crying, grab my hand, and say, "Listen, I'm tired. We really can't do this anymore. We're done. We have to go our separate ways. You do not care about us."

I told her that I believed we would eventually have something meaningful. I told her that I wanted to take care of her and my daughter; being illegal in the US without paperwork, LookClean was my best shot at being the provider I wanted to be.

I would then buy time and tell her that if divorce is what she wanted, we could have a serious talk another day, but I was tired and did not want to talk about divorce. Thankfully, we never really had a serious conversation about divorce.

I remember one morning having a conversation with relatives about the business when I said, "I know that you guys probably think I'm crazy. But this is something I have to do. You guys don't have to understand."

BLEACHED PIZZA

When we were living with my in-laws, I wouldn't touch most of the food. I would eat the bare minimum. I wasn't the one providing. I wasn't the one going grocery shopping. I wasn't contributing. They always made it very clear that I could eat and do whatever I wanted. I would have supper but never second servings.

Most nights, I would go to work hungry. Around two or three in the morning, I would be starving. There were vending machines, but I didn't have money.

To motivate their employees to stay with the company, every Monday they had a huge pizza party. They would buy about twenty extra-large pizzas.

Around four in the morning, the supervisor would ask me to dispose of the remaining pizza in the dumpster. I was too proud to ask for a slice. I would load my trash cart up and go down to the loading dock where the dumpster was located and dispose of all the leftover pizzas. I remember being in the elevator with the pizzas, and it was torture. They smelled so delicious. I would grab a bottle of bleach and pour it on top of every single slice that I could find so I wouldn't be tempted. I knew that around seven in the morning, I would be so hungry that I would end up taking a slice or two. Many times I would go back looking for a slice that I did not cover in bleach, but I knew there would be none.

After disposing of the pizzas, I would sit on the loading dock and call my wife, and we would cry together. It was anger mixed with hunger and so many other emotions at that time. Tears would be pouring from me uncontrollably.

If I had given in to that temptation, I would just be a regular business like any other.

THEY WERE GETTING INTO MY HEAD

People around me started to get into my head, and I started having second thoughts about my business until I decided to make my commitment to the business stronger.

I called a janitorial supplier and asked for $7,500 worth of equipment. I told him I would need about forty-five days to pay it off. Without knowing my financial situation, he said OK.

When everyone around me found out that most of the machines I bought didn't have a use for the account I was cleaning, they thought I had lost my mind. I told them that I did not buy the equipment for the account I had. I bought it for the accounts I will eventually have.

To this day, I still have every single machine that I purchased twelve years ago.

UNIFORM

I mentioned making company shirts with iron-on letters, but there was one big problem. I would be vacuuming and sweating, and the letters would start to fall off.

I would try to stick my letters back on without anyone noticing. I would also take the letters that fell off and put them into my pocket.

That went on for the first few months of the business until we started getting some money, and I was finally able to make professional company shirts.

❖

HUMMER

My wife dropped me off at work one day, and I saw this beautiful Hummer in the parking lot.

I commented that one day, I would have one of those trucks. There was an employee outside who started to laugh, and my wife joined him.

I smiled at him and said, "What? You don't like them?"

He said, "Look at what you're driving—a Ford Focus. Do you know how much these things cost?"

I brushed him off and kept walking. When I got home, I told Trina to never laugh at me again because I would have a brand-new truck one day. She said that she was not laughing at me. She was laughing because she thought that I was funny. I told her it was not.

I said that one day, I would walk into a Chevy dealer and buy a custom-made truck and pay cash for it.

❖

FIRST CHECK

Ninety days and I received my first check. It was a partial payment for the first month of services.

Then another, and another and another came. Financially, I was not doing great, but I was able to stay current with my bills and have a little extra at the end of the month.

At this point, we also started the process of renting an apartment and got out of my in-laws' house.

❖

YOU CAN NO LONGER CLEAN HERE!

When I finally thought all was well, and the business was moving forward, the vice president of the company signed a new contract and, as part of the deal, everyone who worked at the building needed to undergo a background check. This included all vendors and employees.

I knew I would never pass a background check. I did not have a social security number or a driver's license.

I called the manager of the site and just like in Olive Garden, I told her I was an illegal alien and would never pass a background check. I did not have any records, good or bad. She told me I would no longer be allowed into the building.

I told Trina, and she volunteered to quit her job at Bob's and take over the cleaning.

That was a tough decision for Trina to make. She never signed up to be a cleaner. She went to college, and I know for a fact that cleaning is not what she envisioned doing after she graduated. She did it anyway, and subsequently, saved the business!

Trina took care of the cleaning for one month. Shortly after, the company changed management, and I was able to return to the cleaning.

❖

I WOULD LOVE THAT

One day, my wife and I were driving to the bank. Upon arriving, she saw a white Mercedes-Benz. It was a beautiful car and it seemed so far away from anything we could ever achieve.

She told me she absolutely loved the car, and one day she wished she could have one but knew it would probably never happen.

I told her that one day, I would give her a Mercedes. She laughed and said that if I ever bought her one, to please make sure that I did not buy one with the Mercedes emblem sticking out of the hood. I told her it was noted, and I would make sure it did not have the emblem.

HE IS NOT GIVING US THE ACCOUNT

Trina spotted a building being built in Agawam. We had moved out of her parents' house and back into our apartment, which was right around the corner from this new building.

My wife called, and the manager of the building had brushed her off very quickly. My wife is not a salesperson and never wanted to be one. So, once he said no, that was it for her.

Like anything in life, you've got to be persistent. Don't take the first no that someone gives you. Keep on persisting, keep on asking, and eventually, you're going to get a yes.

She kept calling the manager, and eventually, he said yes. We went to a meeting in the new building. He showed us the building and asked us to give him a proposal for cleaning services. I gave him a proposal, and he called my wife to set up another meeting.

Back in Brazil, you may have people next to you laughing, acting like they are your friends and the next thing you know they are stabbing you in the back. You have to learn that a smile doesn't mean friend; that smile could mean quite the opposite.

From a young age, I learned to read people: their body language, tone of voice, eye contact, and other nonverbal cues. Sometimes that was the difference between making it home alive, or not—that's why it was so important to develop those instincts quickly.

When the manager of the new building called to set up a meeting, I asked my wife to transcribe the conversation in detail.

After hearing the entire conversation, I told my wife that he was not going to give us the account. My wife thought I was crazy and asked me to please let it play out and not try to read the future.

THE MEETING

The day of the meeting, we walked into his office. He looked at us, shook our hands, and said, "The very first thing I want to tell you guys is that I'm not giving you the account." I wanted to look at my wife so bad and say I told you so.

He invited us to the conference room. I was twenty-three years old, and my wife was twenty-seven. He said, "You guys are too young. You don't have any experience. You don't have any certifications, any qualifications. But I believe in you guys. You are doing a great job. I'm so impressed with you, I believe in you."

We left his office, and my wife was very disappointed. I was thrilled! For a long time, everyone was calling me crazy and told me I would never make it. For the first time, someone looked me in the eyes and said he believed in me.

CERTIFICATIONS

When I arrived home, I went immediately to my computer and started searching for any certification that I could find for free. I got certified in how to wash hands, how to fold towels, how to move tables, first aid, and so forth. Anything silly I could find, I got it!

After obtaining a certification, I would email it directly to the manager of the new building.

BIG BREAK

One day he called me, and he said, "Anderson, I can see that you are well-qualified now. I'm going to take a chance on you."

We walked through his building, and he said, "Don't ever let me down."

I looked into his eyes and said, "I will never let you down."

What I didn't know was that he was part of a fast-growing real estate development company. At that time, they had ten or eleven buildings; they now have over forty!

We clean every one of their buildings, and they do not pay on time; they always pay early!

The name of that manager is Travis W. He became a good friend and has taught me many lessons throughout the years. I owe a lot of my success to him and will forever be grateful for all he has done to help my business.

❖

A NEW OPPORTUNITY

Travis referred my company to a therapy clinic in Northampton, Massachusetts. Among the many services they offered, they provided therapy to kids. After a couple of weeks of negotiations, they hired my company to clean their Northampton clinic.

There were therapy rooms with several dolls, teddy bears, little soldiers, many different toys. I would clean the entire site perfectly! I would straighten all the papers on the desks. I even bought a ruler and would measure to make sure all was perfect.

Sometimes my wife would call and ask, "What are you still doing there?"

I would say, "I'll be home soon, just one more notebook left to straighten." I would clean it until it was perfect. The cleaning had to be beautiful.

❖

GOING THE EXTRA MILE

I would go a step further. I wanted the little kids who walked into the facility to see it not as a chaotic room; I assumed everything was already chaotic in their lives. I wanted them to step in and say, "Wow!"

There was a dollhouse full of furniture and little tiny pieces. I would fix all of the furniture inside the house. I would put the dolls laying on the bed; all the furniture was organized properly. I would even have the teddy bears hugging each other and the soldiers fighting each other.

The next day the therapist would get on the phone and call me and ask, "Anderson! Who did you have cleaning my site last night?"

At this point, I had a couple of employees cleaning my first account, but I was the one cleaning the therapy clinic. I would tell her, "Well, I don't know. I've gotta look at the schedule."

I was a one-person show, but I never told anybody it was only me. I did not want them to limit the amount of business they would give me.

She would say, "Well, regardless, tell them that they did a beautiful job. When I walked in, it put such a big smile on my face." She would go further and say, "You're not going to believe it, Anderson." I would ask her to tell me. She would tell me about the dollhouse, the little soldiers, and other detailed arrangements.

I was tempted to say, "You forgot the dog I put in the corner hugging the teddy bear," but I contained myself.

Fast forward ten years: their clinic grew rapidly, and we now clean ten of their sites!

ORIGAMI

I signed a new contract with a construction company office. There were no papers for me to fix, no dolls, or other details that children would appreciate. However, I wanted to do more than simply clean. I tried to deliver the "WOW" service!

The owner of the business was an old-school construction guy. How could I impress him beyond doing an excellent job on the cleaning? I thought about buying a bottle of wine, maybe a six-pack of beer, but I thought it would perhaps cross a line.

One day, I had a perfect idea! I bought an origami book on how to fold toilet paper. Every single holiday was a different fold. For Christmas? Santa. Valentine's Day? A big rose. Easter? A bunny.

Sitting on the toilet, the construction guy calls me, and he says, "Anderson! I'm sitting on the toilet and there is a bunny staring at me. What do I do with this thing?"

Bingo! That was the emotion that I was looking for. We built an immediate connection. I got it from him sitting on the toilet, and that was the best reaction that I could ask for.

To this day, my team still folds toilet paper.

❖

WOW GIFT

For every new account we start, we always buy a "WOW" gift for the customer.

The WOW gift is composed of a lovely plant or flowers, a mini toilet, a mini plunger, jelly beans, and a "Welcome to the Family" card.

The WOW gift always left a lasting impression on all our new customers. Sometimes we would sign a $250 per month contract and spend over $100 on their WOW gift.

It was, and still is to this day, about connecting cleaning with emotions. We always go all out, and it has paid dividends.

❖

ANDERSON CLEANING

In 2012, I changed the name of the company from LookClean Commercial Services to Anderson Cleaning.

In the beginning of the business, it was difficult with my accent to say LookClean Commercial Services. People would always ask me to spell it. I would get nervous and the conversations would not flow smoothly—so I thought I would choose something easier.

CHAPTER 7

GOALS

SILVERADO

I n 2012, when we had been in business for five years, I walked into a Chevy dealer. I sat down with a salesperson, and he asked, "What do you want? Which one of our trucks in the lot do you want?"

I said, "No, I don't want anything you have on the lot. I want to build my truck."

He said, "You are going to have to pay to ship."

I said, "That's fine!"

He said, "Why? That's crazy. You can choose something on the lot. You won't have to pay to ship."

I said, "No, I want something custom-made!" We sat at the computer and designed the entire truck.

He informed me that if I spent $5,000 more, I would be able to buy a Corvette for the price I was paying for the truck!

We finished everything, and I bought the truck, and paid cash!

FULFILLMENT?

I now had a brand new black Chevy Silverado precisely the way I wanted. It had cooling seats, heated seats, LED in the back, bed liner, beautiful rims...it was gorgeous!

The moment I sat in the driver's seat and drove off the lot, I called my wife. She was delighted. She asked, "Are you happy?"

I told her, "Not really."

She said, "What? For five years you didn't stop talking about this truck!"

I'm very analytical toward things, so I said, "No, I thought I was going to have this big huge feeling of happiness." But it was almost like a depression. A sense of sadness overcame me.

I had accomplished one of the first goals that I worked hard for, a purpose driven by a guy who laughed at me when I said I would one day have a Hummer, but now I was unhappier than before.

A lot of questions popped into my head. What was next? The business was doing fine, and my only goal was accomplished. Now what? I was not fulfilled, and I thought I would be.

That's when I sat down at the computer to think about what was important to me; to create new goals, something new to focus on and aim for.

One of my new goals was to generate $1 million in sales in one year. Another goal was to buy rental properties and make it a successful side business. But my major goal was to be able to spend more time with my wife and daughters.

Whether you are striving for a new job, more meaningful relationships, or personal enlightenment, I believe you need to want something more in order to live a happy life. The journey towards accomplishing a goal is what gives you real, meaningful satisfaction, not the realization of the goal itself.

MERCEDES

In 2017, I was finally able to buy my wife her dream car. I went to a dealer and bought her a Mercedes-Benz E-350.

There was one problem. My wife hated the Mercedes emblem sticking out of the hood. So I called Mercedes, drove one hour and forty-five minutes, and was able to have the Mercedes emblem removed from the hood and exchanged for a flat emblem that was flush with the hood.

Christmas of 2017, I surprised Trina with the Mercedes. I told her, "Remember the car that you dreamed of, remember ten years back when you said you would love a white Mercedes? Go look outside!"

She cried, hugged me, and explored her new toy.

It was one of the proudest moments of my life.

❖

WAS THE MOTIVATION MONEY?

If you asked if I made money, if I was profitable, the answer would be no! If you divided the time I spent on each account for the money I was making, it would end up being two or three dollars per hour. They weren't paying me to fix the dolls, to straighten the notebooks. They were paying me to clean.

Of course, I needed to pay bills, so I can't lie and say I wasn't working for the money. I was. But it was never my main motivator.

Even when the time I invested wasn't reflected in my pay, I always refused to do just the minimum, or just what I was getting paid for. I believe in doing more than what you are paid for as an investment in your future. I have always believed in connecting emotion with our cleaning, which is why I believe so firmly in delivering the "WOW" factor!

If you do the right thing, the money will always catch up to you eventually. Many think that if they were getting paid more, they would work harder. In my opinion, that's never going to work. Nobody is going to give you more and all of a sudden, you become the CEO. You need to work yourself up to that position by always doing more than is expected of you. The money will follow you there, never lead you there.

CHAPTER 8

MILLION DOLLARS

W hen we reached ten years in business, we hit a huge milestone.

I drove home, called Trina, and informed her we had reached $1 million in revenue. She was so happy, and so was I.

Most businesses never reach the million-dollar mark; others reach it much more quickly. But for us, it was meaningful for so many reasons.

A few years before, we could not find ten cents to buy that ice cream. Now we were generating $1 million in sales.

We sat down on the couch and discussed the beginning of the business and everything we put our family through to get us to a million. It was a special moment for both of us.

CHAPTER 9

IMMIGRATION

L iving illegally makes you fearful of everything. Even if someone else is doing wrong, it makes you afraid to call the police. There was a possibility that I would still be the one getting into trouble at the end and maybe even be deported back to Brazil.

Simple things like going to the post office or opening a bank account become big tasks and very embarrassing at times. I had no identification, so any place that asked for a simple ID, I did my best to stay away from. Trina would be the one obtaining membership cards, going to the liquor store, making returns to stores, and doing any task that required identification, and potentially catching up to my illegal status.

Every time I drove somewhere, I never knew if I would return home. I had no driver's license but never once got stopped by the police. Fear of being deported always caused me to follow the rules precisely and develop some good habits that I carry with me to this day.

After ten years of living in the United States, I finally qualified and had the money to file an immigration waiver to be forgiven for coming to the United States illegally through Mexico.

One of the requirements, after the waiver was approved, was to go back to Brazil and go for an interview in the American consulate. If approved, I would then reenter the United States legally. It was mandatory that the interview be held in Brazil. It was also a fifty-fifty chance that I would return. So, I did not start the process right away.

One day, one of my biggest customers rented one of his buildings to a courthouse. One of the requirements was for everyone who entered the courthouse to undergo an extensive background check. Once again, I was facing the immigration issue.

The customer was a good friend. I called him and told him the truth about my immigration status. At first, he seemed shocked, but soon after he told me he would do whatever it took to help me out. I promised him that I would start the immigration process as quickly as possible, and that's what I did! I hired a lawyer and started the process.

The process included people around me writing reference letters and our family going to a therapist to see what the impact of my being deported would have on our family. All my tax returns had to be up to date. I had to pass an FBI background check. I had to pass an extensive background check in Brazil; I had to undergo intense scrutiny and investigation.

Luckily, since I had moved to the United States, I had always played by the book and never did anything wrong, other than entering the United States through Mexico. I always paid my taxes, I applied to serve in the military, never received a speeding ticket, never got into trouble with the police, always did everything the right way, and lived an honest life.

When the waiver was approved, and the last step was the interview in Brazil, my lawyer called me into her office and told me, "Do not go back." She said that there were a lot of things happening in the political arena, and she did not want to separate me from my family. She said there were no guarantees. I had only a fifty-fifty chance of coming back to the United States. I was surprised by her suggestion. I had already spent over $15,000 on the entire process.

I told her I was going back to Brazil for the interview. She said that I had to undergo a series of blood tests in Brazil, and if they determined that I had any disease, I would not be able to return. She also stated that if I insisted on going back to Brazil for the interview, I should not bring my wife and kids.

My decision was final; I could not live one more day in the United States illegally.

Before going back, I said goodbye to everyone, delegated my business to my key employees and told them that if I did not return, they should run the business, and I would do whatever I could to help them from Brazil.

UNDOCUMENTED

I bought tickets for my wife and kids, and we all flew to Brazil. My second daughter was born five years after my first daughter.

CHAPTER 10

RETURNING TO BRAZIL

When we arrived in Brazil, I was afraid. So much had changed, but so much was the same.

My interview was scheduled for Wednesday afternoon. It was only Sunday. On Monday, I went to have blood drawn and go through all the tests needed to be able to return to the United States. The medical exams were performed, and if anything were wrong, I would learn of it during the interview.

On Wednesday, I kissed my wife and daughters and left for the interview.

At the interview, I prayed silently, asking God to allow me to go back to the United States. I was petrified at the thought of having to stay in Brazil and never returning to the United States. When my name was finally called, I proceeded to a window where the interview was going to be conducted. The gentleman that was conducting the interviews attempted to speak Portuguese with me, but I was so nervous that I could not remember the words. I then changed the interview to English and was finally able to answer his questions. He asked how long Trina and I had been together, where we met, how many kids we had, and several other questions based on my relationship with her. He took his time looking through the paperwork. After a few minutes, which felt like hours, he looked me dead in my eyes and said, "You are approved." He told me that I would need to go back to my hometown and wait for my passport with the visa to return to the United States.

It was one of the best moments of my life! I was so happy! I wanted to scream, jump, cry! When I left the interview, I immediately looked up and thanked God for allowing me to go back to the place I had come to love, to the United States. A great sense of relief overtook me.

Now all the worry was gone and I could not wait to tell my wife and daughters about the approval. When I returned to the hotel, I ran to the room and told Trina and the girls that I was approved to go back to the United States. They were so happy. My daughters drew a card for me saying congratulations. Trina and I looked at each other and with tears coming down our face, we hugged like we had never hugged before. It was like we hadn't seen each other for years. We both knew the significance of that moment. It was one of the most beautiful moments of my life.

I spent over $25,000 and lost fifty pounds from stress during the immigration process. The only thing left to do was to go back to my hometown and wait for the visa to arrive.

Going back to my home town was supposed to be the easiest part of the entire process; however, it become one of the hardest things I had to do. For the first time in ten years, I would have to face my father...my mother...friends that I did not necessarily want to see. I was going back to the place I had escaped from.

So many emotions were going through my head, so many questions: "What if my father starts screaming at me? What if he hits my mother? What if he is aggressive toward my daughters, my wife?" I was angry and ready to face him, but was fearful to expose my wife and daughters to the confrontation that I was anticipating. But I had no options. If I wanted to return to the United States, I had to face my fear and go back to my hometown.

BACK IN MY HOMETOWN

I contacted my brother to come to pick us up from the airport. He was speechless. Up to that point, I had kept the fact that I was going through the immigration process a secret from my brother and parents. I told him not to tell anyone that I was back in Brazil, including my parents.

We stayed in a hotel room, and I asked my brother to gather the entire family, including my uncles, aunties, grandparents, and cousins, and we would surprise them.

My family was super happy to see me. My auntie started to cry, my grandmother gave me a big hug...everyone was genuinely happy. They could not believe that the boy that left over ten years back had now returned with a wife and two beautiful daughters.

However, I felt out of place. I had not spoken with many of them for a decade. I felt that I did not belong there. I was not home! I kept my two daughters and wife next to me at all times and would not take my eyes away from them. I wanted to protect them and make sure they were okay

My family seemed different, they all seemed to have moved on from the past, including my father, and I was still holding on to every single bad memory that I had....and it was affecting the people closest to me. I wasn't the best husband or the best father I could be.

My dad tried to to initiate small talk; he even gave me a hug, which caught me off guard and I reluctantly accepted. I didn't want him touching me. After he touched me, I felt like I needed to take a shower. I felt dirty, disgusted...it was almost like someone had violated me. It was a repulsive feeling.

The confrontation I had been predicting that I would have with my father never happened. He did not mention the past and did not show any signs of aggression.

The visa arrived; I went back to the United States. But I felt like I still had unfinished business back in Brazil. I had to tell my father how I felt about him and confront him about the things he did to me and put me through.

BACK IN THE USA LEGALLY

Entering the United States legally was an incredible experience. I could not help but think about walking the desert, crossing the Rio Grande, jumping off the train, and seeing the American flag for the first time. It was a humbling experience. I felt part of the culture and felt that I had arrived home. I could look people in the eyes and felt equal to everyone. I was no longer living in fear.

One of the first things I did was to get my social security card. After that, I got my driver's license, gun license, any and every document that I could not obtain before due to my illegal status.

To this day, now and then I pull my driver's license out of my wallet and look at it. So much goes through my head when looking at my driver's license. After eleven years of having no license, it was like I obtained a college degree!

I was now living in the United States, legally. There was no longer the fear of being deported or being stopped by the police. I was on my way to becoming an American citizen.

But the fact that I had not confronted my father when I was in Brazil was bothering me tremendously. I needed to go back. I needed to let him know how I felt.

❖

BACK IN BRAZIL - THE SECOND TIME

I asked Trina to go back to Brazil with me because I needed to talk with my father. I told her that when I confronted my dad, he would likely start to scream and become aggressive. I told her that, when that happened, we would leave and go to a hotel to enjoy the rest of the trip. I just needed to say to him how I felt.

When I saw my dad, I told him, "Listen, you don't know how abusive you were, how aggressive you were, how much you hurt me." To my surprise, my dad did something he never had done before, the one thing I did not expect him to do…he started to cry. I was not prepared for that. I was prepared for many reactions, but not for him crying.

We hugged, and I decided at that moment to move on. It was like I was released from a prison. I was free for the first time in over thirty years! I decided to forgive him!

Forgiveness did not justify his actions or mean what my father did was right. It only means I was choosing to let go of the hatred so that the pain could no longer control my life. You forgive that person who hurt you—not for his or her sake—but the sake of your own mental and physical health and wellbeing!

Now the only thing left to do was to go back to the United States and work towards my citizenship, and finally be able to call the United States my forever home!

BECOMING A CITIZEN

After I obtained my green card, I had to wait two years to be able to apply for citizenship.

Going through the citizenship process was excellent. I learned a lot about the United States, the place I am happy to call home!

At the citizenship ceremony I was surrounded by people who had supported me. My wife and two beautiful daughters were there, and you could see on their faces how proud they were. My father-in-law, mother-in-law, sister-in-law and brother-in-law were all there to congratulate me as well. They had all been a big part of my immigration journey and knew the struggles I had faced. Travis, the manager who gave me my first big break in business, was also there to celebrate. Travis's coworkers gave me an American flag that I cherish to this day. It is one of the best gifts I have ever received.

I spent a little over $30,000 on my entire immigration process, including the citizenship, but I would have paid double or triple if that's what was needed.

Becoming a citizen of the United States was a dream come true. I am proud to be an American!

CHAPTER 11

TODAY

Today, Anderson Cleaning employees over one hundred team members. We service over one hundred job sites. The company generates well over $1 million per year, and we own a 10,000-square-foot building in West Springfield, Massachusetts.

I also accomplished my goal to start a real estate company that has invested in several rental properties. All the properties that I own are paid off and generate a substantial amount of income.

I say this not to brag about myself. I want to show everyone that if a kid who grew up the way I grew up, who came from Brazil through Mexico without a dollar to his name, who lived illegally in the country for eleven years without a social security card or driver's license, can make it, you can as well!

CHAPTER 12

PLAN TO SUCCEED

One thing that has contributed to my success was learning to write down everything and plan the days, the weeks, the year. Everything that happens is first planned on paper. After that, I can move on to the execution of it.

I plan all my days and weeks ahead of time. I also begin the day by writing down one thing that I am grateful for. In the evenings, I review and write down my wins, the lessons learned, and take a look at the following day. This happens seven days per week.

My goals are also in writing. If you aim at nothing, you will hit it every time. So, having goals on paper gives you a direction; it guides you to shape your days and weeks toward achieving the goals.

Remember, you do not need a perfect goal; goals can always change. You need to get started and give your life some direction.

THE RIGHT PEOPLE NEXT TO YOU

I have always worked long hours, and for the first five years I skipped every holiday with my family, which included working on Christmas, Thanksgiving, and other holidays and special occasions. I paid a considerable price, and those are memories I will never get back with my daughters and wife.

Trina always supported me and encouraged me. She understands that work is a big part of my life, and I am not fulfilled unless I am being more and doing more.

I remember telling Trina when the business started that if I reached $100,000 in sales, I would settle down and be home more. She told me she wanted to believe it, but knew it was not going to happen.

I reached $100,000 in the first two years, and she was right. I work more today than I worked at the beginning of the business.

If Trina had not supported LookClean and me, then Anderson Cleaning would never have happened. She encouraged me and pushed me up when I needed it the most.

In order to attract and keep the right people next to you, in business and in life, you need to have a good understanding of your

Core Values. We all have them, and your Core Values dictate the type of people you attract.

In my business, my Core Values are:

- Do The Right Thing
- Make Money
- Have Fun
- Deliver WOW Service
- Follow The Anderson Way

So when we hire, we look for those Core Values. If someone likes to work for a place that cuts corners, they are breaking our Core Value: Do The Right Thing, and therefore will not be a good fit. If someone likes a formal business and does not like to have fun, they are not a good fit! That is one of the reasons Anderson Cleaning has been so successful.

The same is true in your personal life. Stop and think about who you are and the Core Values you have. You are likely attracting people with the same Core Values. One great thing is that we all can choose our Core Values; we do not need to accept the ones we have. We can consciously change them and they become mini goals to aim for.

CHAPTER 13

YOU CAN DO IT!

The United States is a place of opportunity; there are no limits to what you can do or how far you can go. You, and only you, set your limits.

I strongly believe that anyone can be successful. Whatever your idea of success is, however, there will be a price to pay. I do not believe in balance. If you want something badly enough, that is what you will focus on. Other areas of your life will consequently be neglected and won't receive as much attention as they should. Does that sound crazy? Maybe it is...or maybe it's just true.

The people around you have their own agendas and fears, and sometimes they will tell you that something is not possible. This is not because they do not want to see you succeed, but because they believe it is not possible. Because they have not done it, they don't think anyone else can.

Sometimes people around you want to protect you, and they will unintentionally push you down because they don't understand the drive you have to succeed even when it's a risk to pursue your dreams.

Some people, like me, have ghosts in their pasts. Mine are still haunting me to this day, but I fight against them every single day. If I give my parents credit for the bad stuff that happened to me, I have to give them credit for my business. I have to give them credit for everything I've achieved! The good and the bad made me the person that I am today, and I am thankful to my parents and everyone who played, and still plays, a part in this forever-evolving story.

It was not easy getting to the place I am today; it was a journey and still is. I am thirty-four years old, and there is so much more I want to accomplish.

I do not have a college degree, nor did I finish high school. At one point I thought those were things that would hold me back, but they are the very things that pushed me to the place I am today.

There was no Plan B. I had only Plan A. So, there was no option but to make it work. Many people will tell you not to burn any bridges, but I firmly believe from time to time, you need to pour gasoline on the entire bridge and burn the crap out of it! You need to be sure that you can never cross that bridge again, and there is no option but to figure out another way.

I do not believe in safety nets. I believe in jumping and then figuring out where you are going to land. I am proud to have landed in a position where I can influence and impact lives. It is possible... believe and work hard toward it!

This is my story. Thank you for reading. If you take anything from this book, please believe that in life, anything is possible. Believe in yourself, even if everyone around you doesn't. Run your race!

God bless the USA

THANK YOU

A huge thank-you to the fine people that made this book possible. I could not have done it without you!

A special thank you to Adrianna Gomes, who helped type half of the book and also made some corrections.

A big thank you to my wife, Trina Gomes, for supporting me and making many grammar changes. I love you!

Thank you to my team member, Mary-Hope Beaulac, for making the story flow better.

Thank you to Joey Swain and Mary Klaes who spent an entire weekend helping to edit the book.

Thank you to Bethany Denton, my final editor, who helped pull all the pieces of my story together.

Illustrations by William Black